MODERN,
AGE,
&C.

RAYMOND RAMCHARITAR

MODERN,
AGE,
&C.

PEEPAL TREE

First published in Great Britain in 2020
Peepal Tree Press Ltd
17 King's Avenue
Leeds LS6 1QS
UK

© Raymond Ramcharitar 2020

All rights reserved
No part of this publication may be
reproduced or transmitted in any form
without permission

ISBN 13: 9781845234614

CONTENTS

Modern

1: The Modern Angel	11
2: A Modern Virgil	13
3: The Modern Mind	
Seizure	15
Ward 54	16
Xanax	19
4: The Modern Caribbean	21
5: The Modern City	30
6: Modern Blackness	31
7: Modern Love	33
8: The Modern Poet	35
9: The Modern Island	36
10: Modern Journalism	40
11: A Modern Walden	42
12: Modern Exile	44
13: The Modern Parent	45
14: Modern Myth	48
Ekalavya	
Caliban	
15: Modern Death	59

Age, &c.

16: Birthday Boy	65
17: The Approach	67
18: Midway	69
19: 30 to T2	71
20: Letter to 25	74
21: An Imperfect Ending	77
22: Two Elegies	
(i) *The Monk and the Buddha*	79
(ii) *The Lark of Darkness*	82

23: The Divine Body at Prayer	85
24: The Unfinished	86
25: The Starship Enterprise	87
26: Unrequited	88
27: An Island in the Sea	90

For my daughter, Aurora,
and
in memory of my mother,
Dhanmatee Ramcharitar
(1948 – 2017)

ACKNOWLEDGEMENTS

The quotations, some in quotes or italics, and some not, used in the poems "The Modern Caribbean" and "The Monk and the Buddha" come from Derek Walcott's essays, "The Muse of History" and "What the Twilight Says: An Overture", collected in *What the Twilight Says*; Vidia Naipaul's essay on Trinidad in *The Middle Passage*, Sir W Arthur Lewis's Address to University College of the West Indies (Mona) Graduands in 1961, published in the Trinidad *Guardian* on June 15, 1961; and Carolyn Cooper's Op-Ed "Who is Jamaica" in the *New York Times* on August 5, 2012.

The translation of Ekalavya was derived using Ramesh Menon's contemporary rendering of the *Mahabharata* as well as K Mohan Ganguli's Victorian translation of the same work.

The sculpture depicted on the cover was done by Guyanese artist, Winslow Craig, and is reproduced with his permission.

MODERN

Muse, put your breast in my mouth
If you want me to sing.
(Fuck the Muse.)
   — Ovid, via Frederick Seidel

1: THE MODERN ANGEL –
FORMERLY KNOWN AS SINEAD O'CONNOR
(For Annabelle Sooklal)

Transfixing, the shining heart-shaped face, the dreamy
eyes, the tawny hair, bristling, skull-short,
but eclipsed by the voice, belting out a steamy
"Nothing compares to u," a bluesy retort
to love, that its power over you was strong
but not complete: you'd sometimes lose your way
but find it again, and that beautiful tongue
would find different sounds and music to say
those words that waken gold in the bluest heart.
It was that voice that brought me another world
as I listened on an island, a world apart,
where love was ruthlessly carnal; a story told
by slack-mouthed mummers, satyrs in crude disguise
whose weapon was vice, whose quest to decivilise.

*

But more than the song: the sight of the fierce Angel
who scaled the modern Babel to glare at God,
reminding him of the innocence of the manger
and its chief strangler: the vicar of his synod,
whose picture you ripped asunder as the world gasped
at televised heresy, but refused to see,
beyond the unbent knee, the Papal clasp
that sealed the truth of Christ on earth: misery.
The Christian veneer of worldliness cracked
and St Sinatra swore righteous violence,
to spank and smack and kick your ass, for attacking
the stony fortress of innocent suffering's silence,
certain the bloodstained hassocks would be cleaned
in the holy laundry of the Magdalene.

*

The laity believe their angels are made
of heavenly substance: their skin ethereal,

bodies bathed in halo that will never fade,
and minds of magical material
that grosser creatures cannot discern. But no:
when they lay down the flaming sword and shield
angels are fragile beings who do not know
the things the world, and its god, choose to conceal.
They have children, whom they love, and fail and lose.
They, who in battle, can see with blazing sight, are blind
to the slow unravelling of the restless mind.
They see the angry blemish as a bruise
and not a cancer, and sometimes try to barter
with fate, who, as they fade, makes a martyr.

*

It's been decades since that starry face first stared
accusingly through the television screen.
There've been husbands, children, a scrappy career.
The Church in Rome's been judged and found obscene;
accusing eyes are everywhere, and anger's
the millennial lingua franca. The restless mind
is soothed by drugs, and thought to be a danger
to its owner. The revolution's been refined,
and you've realigned: Sinead is now Shuhada.
The plot has changed from crusade to intifada;
and now, your halo's eclipsed by a dark cloth.
A star has taken a moon to plight her troth.
seeking the blaze of an unknowable father,
O Angel of Light, you have become a moth.

2: A MODERN VIRGIL

At times, as the curfew tolls the tiresome knell,
I yearn the stately strangeness of Frederick Seidel.

As homeostatic ice sheets dwindle
and snowy dreams become brindled

by stains of slushy meltwater
that covers islands like muddy mortar,

I glide to London, Claridge's, through Europe on the Eurostar,
or Iran, before the mullahs, to sport with the Shah,

alight in the most expensive hotels in the world
mixing local knowledge with Cuervo Gold.

But it's not the easy excess, the droll deftness
of his pen, nor intimations of the Milton's Hefner,

whose bunnies pout at publishing parties
and smilingly straddle bespoke Ducatis,

whose consorts are pure aristo roses
with soigné necks and Grecian noses,

who's a feast for petulant helots:
Feminists & "woke" Twitter zealots.

It's beneath the careful nihilism;
the familiar rhythm

of a bearish heart
that lives apart,

a Sybarite
bringer of light,

A restive mind
on an island designed

by cruelty, for lust —
Manhattan, Barbados —

where past and present converge
he's a recrudescent Virgil,

weightless, but heavy with wisdom,
shared in narcotic idiom,

with a glint in the cloudy eye
that winks with the stars of our common sky.

3: THE MODERN MIND

(i) *Seizure*

It's not the sight of your stricken body,
you think, as you watch it flailing.
It's what it does
now that you no longer have sole custody:
it's a child again, a yearling
in hopeless distress
watching its mother behind the milky screen
in a grey field
her fate sealed
by the imprint of the axe in her death dream.

Do animals dream?
Do they scream?

A head quivers like a baroque rose on a slim stem
then goes rigid
as the skull is wrenched
to slap the bedclothes.
A back arches and toes clench,
arms twist like windmills,
digits attack the bed like hammer drills.
The spark
of consciousness gutters,
and all is dark.

Then a panorama. The world skims by a Checker
cab window, past a flatiron building near Chelsea
where Broadway cuts Fifth at the knee.
Dali, balancing a cigar beneath his razor-
thin moustache, stolidly mutters "Baedeker"
as a man in a straw boater and white blazer
murmurs: "Surrealism is so passé, don't you agree"?

(ii) *Ward 54*

You return slowly, after you've been undone.
The body glitches, the eyes flicker.
                                        The sun
has been sucked into a fragile fluorescent tube,
its gold transmuted to silver, a sickly nude
descending a staircase.
                            The thoughts that zoom
too fast for neural transit explode.
                                        A room
comes into focus: a row of steel-framed beds
with broken bodies in them; forlorn black heads
and limbs submerged in mottled sheets lie still.
A tremor as your own body convulses to spill
its pent-up anguish. An hourglass dripping lead.
A slackened jaw. A molten pain in the head.

You grope for the last coherent thought: *the fucking
public hospital*, before the jaw locked,
and vision's circuit relayed to the third eye,
or the forebrain, or the purple pre-dawn sky,
where the body reappears as its wolves
howl at the baleful moon as it dissolves.

                *

Morning in the garden of non-being:
the cameras and nurses doze, unseeing.
They turn up the radio at 4 am when the shift
changes. They need the soca screams to lift
their droopy spirits that early in the morning.
Fuck the helpless patients. Silence and fawning
are for the private sector. Here lie the broken,
the vulgar, the wage slave, the pretender whose token
life, a journey to the bourgeois Mecca,
didn't come with insurance or a Baedeker.

This is the apogee, Ward 54;
this is ground zero for the shattered core,
where the 'I' it took a lifetime to build
lies in pieces in a modern landfill.
*
The beauty of everything now being frozen
is the clarity of everything you'd chosen
till then; the mind's machinery's laid out
without the customary shield of doubt;
and causes are so clear, almost mundane.
You want to explain: it's just the restless brain
staging a minor revolt, to overthrow
linear logic's grim politburo
by imprisoning the body, demanding ransom
of a lost time when it was young and handsome.

It's minor; that's the point you want to make
to the white-coated interns who trot in the wake
of the chief consultant, whose time's too valuable
to peer too deeply into the minds of the rabble,
and waves the malaise away with neurology.
You sense the impatience with psychology.
*
Even semiconscious, some things are plain,
like the pursed lips and eyes which show disdain
to the notion that complex lives could exist
outside consulting suites in private practice.
The wondrous ego contrives a neural path
for thought to travel from the enflamed heart,
but, as usual, a translational mistake:
you can see them, but somehow cannot break
the surface of sludge sitting like crepe
over your burbling mind. Like a caged ape
the force of a broad chest and tree-trunk arms
are useless before these silent wide-eyed lambs
staring down impassively, and you wonder:

What do they see?
                     A mind now ripped asunder,
an aging body broken through constant attrition
from relentless steel-edged waves of the modern condition.

Somewhere, on the floor of a shallow lake
the lesson filters through: *What do you make*
of this: *Male subject, at forty-eight,*
unhappy, unhealthy, a failure, overweight?
And you think: *that about sums it up.* It behooves
you to remind them: *don't forget unloved.*

                     *

Within hours, days, this will have been submerged
to the unfathomable depths of the primal urge.

Life will paper over this mental disjunction
and call the bridge Modern Functional.

(iii) *Xanax*

The floor is about one degree off its axis.
A hum: a thickening in the ears; was it always
there? Forks seem suddenly strange to touch.
Pop songs make no sense. The roads begin
to curve at random, like a foreign syntax invading
your tongue. And people become impossibly far –
distant just when you need them to be near.
Ordinary slips from apprehension; your grasp
and jaws slacken. Have you always been so alone?
Who sprayed clear-coat over the conversation?
What is the atomic weight of geranium?
Weighing atoms seems like a strange idea.
> *The heart still seems to work;*
> *autonomic; auto-pilot;*
> *the software works in the dark;*
> *it is wrapped in a neural knot;*
> *it carries its own spark*
> *above the brain's moist murk.*

Meanwhile, back in the present – there is no present:
a lag: everything's a few seconds behind
and slim dark ropes are vining limbs. Nerves
are firing randomly at ghosts; the shots
ricochet. *Sound*: another sense to manage.
It's all too much to manage. Are you the swimmer
who begins to think: "Let him go and save
myself", not knowing you're the one drowning?
Waves of ice-cream ripple from memory
creating cross currents. The tide is rising.
Are we at the beach now? Sand, white and dry;
water, dark and churning. What is a Baedeker?

*

It is deflating that such a little thing
could tame a giant beast. A tiny feast
of orange flecks that could salvage the wrecks
from the brutal shoals in the brain's roiling folds.
Couldn't genius evolution find a solution
to Thanatos, or acedia, its precursor ghost,
that reset the clock without the final hemlock?
Couldn't the modern condition offer remission
outside consuming, desiring, neural rewiring?

And *there*, with no fuss, clarity, at last
returns; the floor re-tilts, reality recast.
The clocks and footsteps return to regular patterns.
The Stepford wives return and chase the slatterns.
It's right again: precise and punctual,
fluorescent lights make darkness functional.

4: A REPORT TO THE ACADEMY: THE MODERN CARIBBEAN
(For Bridget Brereton)

"In passing: May I say that all too often, men are betrayed by the word 'freedom'. And as freedom is counted among the most sublime feelings, so the corresponding disillusionment can also be sublime."

— Kafka

1
Noble Sirs, you do not know me, and I won't
bore you with a résumé; I'll just say,
in case any of you should take affront
at this intrusion to your college, to allay:
I am what's left; the remains of the day:
Eschaton: after the chains and whips,
a cheerful, indigenous apocalypse.

You might well ask, but why now? Or, what's new?
The simplest answer is most morbid, but apt:
you're all departed and dead, the sea's still blue
and the brutes in charge, and those they rule, are enrapt
on tiny azure screens, and still entrapped
by Mephistopheles, in binary code,
barrelling down that ancient, slippery road.

It's an unnerving moment in these islands –
which Vidia, had he stayed, might have called
An area of darkness, on whose tepid sands
Derek found himself stunned, his metres stalled,
borrowing Spoiler's lament: *I wanna fall*,
to echo Vidia's dismay at these slave ports –
these islands, these imperial afterthoughts.

Sir Arthur, economic development
is an old joke among the bureaucracy

in the IMF's semi-serious department.
"Consociational democracy"
has been deposed by a grinning adhocracy,
by the Sinons who ascend from the masses,
cheered on by the jawbones of grobian asses.

Derek, Vidia, poetry and prose
these days are "spoken words" and Facebook screeds,
not like the days when men could come to blows
over taunts like "Mimic Man", the dubious deeds
of heroic Shabine, or jousts on donkey steeds.
Your deaths brought murmurs of spurned prophets, but lacked
the traction of Olatunji on X Factor.

2
Sir Arthur, our Elijah, you could see
the problems early on, and devoted your life
to spinning gold from straws of morbid fancy.
Like how to harness unlimited labour and strife
in these plant-nations, where overseers stifled
the proles and primed them for the doctor kings,
colonial Davids with backfiring slings.

But the rigid labour curve never wavers.
The supply's endless, and Capital's relentless. It seems
you underestimated the former slavers'
alacrity for foiling Fabian dreams;
and to quell proletarian socialist screams
with Doctor politics, and the ballot nostrum,
so master-servant games remained zero-sum.

The malaise is wide and deep. Guyana's found
oil, has land, and gold, but the human divide
refuses to heal. Its people gasp and flounder

in the midst of plenty, and fed the "development" bromide,
respond wittily with suicide.
The tribal nature surreally resists science,
enthralled by sorcery, cults, the nationalist séance.

Trinidad has murdered its black goose,
and its irrational exuberance
now sobered, contemplates the carbon noose.
It's traded the festive for a restive dance
as it prepares itself for commercial romance,
and removes its Carnival masque and eyeliner
to drop to its knees to service imperial China.

Barbados is in trauma; the discipline
and social order, your panaceas, have failed.
Its dollar reels, its industry's supine
as fickle tourist caravels have sailed
to other seas. The IMF has quailed,
and demanded devaluation, making it trample
the social contract that was our shining example!

Should I go on? St Vincent exports ganja,
St Lucia cannot meet its Nobel Laureate
quota, Antigua-Barbuda is in danger
of extinction, battered to a state insensate
by Nature itself, cocking an eyebrow to berate
the temerity of rising above their station,
from patchwork tribe to Potemkin Village nation.

So here's the crux: *the idea of the island
amidst continents*, the absurdity, the scale;
whatever could possess a hundred thousand
to launch a wooden canoe, and hope to trail
an ocean liner – a minnow stalking a whale?
Cyprinids have their kingdoms, to be sure,
but carp do not cavort in behemoths' spoor.

This founding paradox – *nationalism* – crafted
a mob of vices, which conspired to live,
and now are in revolt: *fifty years after
Independence, we must revise our fictive
national motto, and reject the myth of
multicultural assimilation*.
The first grunt of a new myth of creation.

That's Carolyn Cooper, in the *New York Times*
speaking for Jamaica. While natives bicker
about remittances and gruesome crimes,
and local parliaments and power grids flicker,
she heralds the rise of the new Africa,
where *our science, music and language are African*
so Western history and culture must be stricken.

Sixty years ago, Derek upbraided
"revolutionary poets" for this
kind of thing: traducing Perse, and raiding
Césaire for convenient bits, to piss
on history, evict Europe. The twist
is that the revolution is now history,
its slogans sculpted into dogma at UWI.

Europe's in retreat, and you would think
after so many generations, the dust
would have settled, the suffocating stink
diffused. But no: that creeping animus
survives in paroxysms of hateful lust.
The Arabs, Chinese, the other ethnic atoms,
spin on, waiting to trigger ancient bombs.

The interloper Indians – they remain
bemused by global Bollywood as they veer
between East and West Indies. Their epics' refrain
drowned by steely drums, they squint in the glare

of the nationalist flare, painfully aware
that Dharma cannot restrain the majority
fear of recalcitrant minority.

Oh, Sir Arthur, a stab at sanity –
*the image of a tolerant, well-trained,
sensible people* – provokes vanity
for its perversion. The Carnival has drained
the brains, plantation scars remain ingrained,
leaving, as Trollope and Vidia sadly concurred,
no "people" here, in the true sense of the word.

3.
Perhaps, Sir Arthur, in the Communist
hysteria, you made the mistake of misreading
Marx, as the clerisy did, through the mist
of Cold War propaganda – the sly kneading
of desire, markets, and divinity to feed
frenzy – to cast him as Christendom's vulture,
while currying capital's Trojan Horse: culture.

Your early theory of economic growth
was flawed for this, like Newton's universe,
as capital, obsessed with its profit girth,
sullies perfect markets and skews commerce.
You ignored the impish thing which would reverse
progress for profit: the imperfect *animal spirit* –
a gap that yawned for decades till Shiller filled it.

And that rogue variable, that human factor,
has spread like cancer through the vital organs
of these islands, rewriting peasant scripts, enacting
seamy psychodramas, where speech is slogans
and bloody plots find climax in the morgues.
When Vidia and Derek came of age
the recurring revenge plot had become the rage.

But by the moment independence rolled
around, I think you'd grasped the whole design;
from India in '47, then the Gold
Coast, the diasporas turned to align,
and sought Her Majesty's leave to withdraw, resign
from Empire, so each could have a little fief
where, like her, they could be monarch for life.

The trifling questions of exports, the fate of small
economies, were dismissed as atavism
in the thrall of the wicked empire's dying fall,
as trilling manifestoes took optimism
for natural resource, and its product: nationalism.
But what to eat? How to live without trade?
The fledgling parliaments tittered, but remained unswayed.

You saw it, and warned the Mona graduands
in '61 about *false nationalism*
that has persuaded us that the steelband's
a significant contribution to music. The schism
found its perfect form: faux naturalism
on behalf of the morbidly oppressed: the sick
can be cured, hunger and dissent fed, with music.

They sought to politically educate
the peasant, but leave him intellectually
unsoiled, wrote Derek from Trinidad. They equated
calypso and poetry: so Sparrow is Shelley,
the slave is now savant, conceptually.
Two generations on, Carnival monarchy
reigns still, and culture is anarchy.

And it's here, Noble Sirs, your trains of thought
creak to their termini. To a man, you were
children of Arnold; but millennium's brought
the best that's been thought and said, your miracle cure

to everyone, everywhere, but the masses demur,
preferring to consume the vilest vices
and close their eyes to the backdrop of crisis.

It's the time of the photogenic demagogue
whose image is endlessly reproduced:
the beautiful felon, the jet-setting rogue
beguile the desperate, who, free and confused,
now scry beguiling screens for deliverance. Unused
to luxury, or pleasure on demand,
they quietly yearn the patriarch's iron hand.

And they're returning: Hitler, Stalin, Mao,
in every corner, you see their simulacra
in Twitter and IG feeds, which only allow
the brightest, the most charismatic faker –
the dictator rules a continent or an acre.
From Rome to Rupununi, it's not anomaly;
Bokassa, Burnham; Mussolini, Manley.

4
A final paradox must be explored
in querying the fates of these tiny states.
My Lords, the local future is abroad.
Once we discard the dogma which obligates
the peasant to be bound to his squires' estates
and grant him leave to move as he desires,
we loose him, finally, from tribal wires.

In this, lower orders outsmart the upper crust:
they assessed their lot early on, and saw
the smarter strategy was exodus.
While nationalists knocked on the imperial door
the proles perused immigration law,
and as new nations surveyed themselves and blushed
there was barely room to stand on the *Windrush*.

So infinite labour found welcoming stalls
inside imperial walls. Bizarre to reflect
on it: after centuries of the whip, it galls
the national mind, this Freirean effect:
where abused find the abusers and genuflect.
(Though independence polls in Jamaica still glean
the majority thinks it was better with the Queen.)

So now, generations on, the leavers'
numbers equal those who chose to remain.
And here appears one of those mischievous
mysteries religion smirks to explain:
Another Caribbean exists: the dissembled brain
coalesced a body in a northern manger,
leaving the original as its doppelganger.

And embedded in the heart of the old empire,
an archipelago waits to be shaped and primed
to replant the branches uprooted from the mire
into more hopeful soil, a paradigm
where the fruit isn't poisoned by history's slime.
And as plot twists and deus ex machinas go,
here's the Caribbean's back-up, its 2.0.

This is to say, most Noble Sirs, the narrow
interpretation of this inchoate moment
finds the experiment failed: history's arrow
flies off its mark, order falls to ferment,
the lands go fallow, the chattel prepare for interment.
But a wider gaze sees the panorama,
and the instant, a sordid scene in a longer drama.

It remains to be seen whether the Caribbean
motif will grow into significance,
or flicker and disappear from the vast screen;
whether its treasures will sharpen into nuance

or remain trifles, consumed in a greedy glance.
The terrain is, as always, quickly shifting
and islands, alone, remain helplessly drifting.

5: THE MODERN CITY

Its patron saint is Luisa Calderon,
born in history's brothel, she was tortured
by heroic Picton, its father and founding demon,
thus sketching the deep drama of its future:
a spectacle for a tourist spectator.
Ecce Port of Spain: a recurring dream
of hope confronting its natural predator:
venery – its psyche's most enduring theme.
Today, the waterfront is lined with blazing
signs that point to wealth, and a herald a brazen
Church whose dogma's a single word: *rejoice*.
Its eyes glisten, singing hoarsens its voice,
and revelry spreads like tumours as merchants, bankers
waltz around sewers, through ghosts with steaming chancres.

6: MODERN BLACKNESS

We were born to chiaroscuro –
the swash of a war of light and shade
whose cruel colour scheme we follow
still in dreams: where heroes are played
by actors of ochre, pink and gold
with sea-blue eyes, their lips like fresh-
cut apricots, and voices that unfold
silvery music within the flesh.

Our darkness suffused the Gothic grotesque
whose moody colours were thick and bleak,
its characters tragic, a dark burlesque:
the misshapen brute, the hybrid freak.
Not angel nor sprite, our tribal lore
inverted the heroic scene:
Caliban, the Minotaur,
the Sudra, Mulatto, the Bandit Queen.

Today the palette has changed its tones
and the dark themes can now run through
the lightest dreams without the moans
of soiling beauty's natural hue.
Yet in the mingling lurks defeat:
in blackness resides vital absence;
it seems somehow unseemly, a retreat
from destiny, to deny essence
to gratify momentary grief.

In nature, the dark void is threshold
to vistas whose door-price is a brief
moment of negation: the bold
purging of memory and fear
as consumed fuel, temporal dross
which must be ritually cleared

to lighten the mind to leap across
the unknown to the new paradigm,
where different rules have been set,
where human fates do not mime
the shades of nature's blameless palette.

7: MODERN LOVE

The Game of Love, as Santana, featuring
Michelle Branch, reveals it, is played
by drinking long kisses and singing
through lonely bedroom walls, which shimmer and fade,

freeing the oval face to flutter through
the barrio's innards, its main street,
its dinky supermarkets, the blue
lanes and crannies where lips and eyes can meet

below the elevated train's arches,
defying veils across the ground
-floor windows from where loneliness watches.
So the game is complicated, but not profound.

Its rules are flexible and its board is every-
where: the street, the air, tenements
that look up to chase reveries
and escape the barrio's sewers and pavements.

It's a dilemma: one who meditates
on the haunting lemon-slice of the voice,
a trail of breadcrumbs to the gates
of hope, is not a stranger to the joys

of the game, but a maladroit, who gets
mugged in lonely alleys and streets,
who hums the wrong tune and always forgets
it's a game, suffering inglorious defeats.

So, no knights errant on YouTube. Just George
Michael, Sade, and UB 40.
But no one offers their heart to the forge,
and no one feels the moment as they ought to

except for the hapless comic book Quixote
tilting at dull-eyed Dulcineas
and mixing the textures of lamb and goat
with the scales of iron-jawed dragon slayers.

8: THE MODERN POET

Shelley was a bounder, Pope a troll,
Byron bedded his half-sister,
yet poetry made them whole.

Is any creature so sad as the frontier poet?
A minister to savage Babbits
who loathe him, and lavishly show it.

Auden was appalling, Yeats a fool
for love, and Eliot hated Jews,
but poetry let them rule.

The Muses he evokes have hearts of rock.
To those ears, poems are blasts of sand
which stony eyes just mock.

Stevens was a lawyer, the sublime Marvell
was Cromwell's poodle, and Pound was mad,
yet poetry spared them hell.

He seeks the sublime, but finds the sand and rain.
He dreams of touching the frontier's heart.
He fails. He cannot explain.

9: THE MODERN ISLAND

"...the ocean
stares right past us as though
no one here was worth drowning..."
— Auden

And finally, penance
for independence:
a punch-line forms
in the roar of storms;

one of those delayed
drops, by five decayed
decades. But it came,
and they couldn't complain

it disappointed,
as it anointed
the tiny nations
with salty libations.

They could've been foolish
and stayed with the British,
and like Sint Marteen
looked for European

rescue. But no.
They chose to go
it alone. To stand
on their own land

and fly their flag –
their muddy rag –
their fears allayed
by Caricom aid.

The fraternal pact
in case of attack
by man or nature,
or caricature.

No stone on Barbuda
still rests on another.
And Dominica
is flayed; is weaker

than a newborn,
just-orphaned fawn.
Their parliaments
are empty tents.

The only talk
is the sound of the folk
calling to Ogun,
who remains stunned

by the force dour
Prospero conjured,
that melted concrete
like grains of wheat.

Is self-rule too much
for these small duchies?
The old bromide
of national pride

must wear a little thin
when that dark skin
stretches on bones
and rests on stones.

Maybe it's time
to clear the grime
of Calibanism
from Prospero's prism?

The Westminster Model
is silly twaddle,
bending sinister
on the Prime Minister

whose house is rubble,
whose face is stubble.
His hearth was crushed
but his faith's untouched

in promises from
his Caricom,
as Puerto Rico,
also stricken,

tweets to northward
and national guard
regiments muster —
despite the bluster

of their commander,
his eerie candour,
his mania, mixed
with fear of Hispanics.

And without fail
the boats set sail
bearing relief,
assuaging grief.

While in the south
is a slack-mouthed
daze, at the mystery
of spiteful history.

10: MODERN JOURNALISM

"The warm front is now a tropical depression."
The mocha-coloured weather girl's breasts
bulge obscenely, but that's just image compression.
Local TV doesn't have the budget for visual feasts
like CNN, where proportions are human and they speak
a whole language, not creole patois
covered in phony syntax, and smiles that reek
of the empty island scent of *je ne sais quoi*.

The depression moves across the archipelago
at a leisurely pace. Drains become rivers;
the garbage dredged from below assaults the imago
of détente with Nature. The civic lie shivers –
and that's just the weather.
                              Now it's back to
the anchor; the illusion retakes command:
"This video from social media shows a man being hacked
by another as he begs for mercy." A severed hand,
a neck, or missing teenage girl whose selfie
screamed "Save me!" before her body evaporated.
Now in international news: The blade isn't as stealthy
as the oil price, which, as light as thick air, dissipated.

Then the parting blessing: bullet-ridden bodies in a ditch,
slit throats, child abuse, the woman with six children
living in the bleachers of an abandoned cricket pitch,
her helpless rage, her fear-hope that someone would kill them.

Yet somewhere, a caramel-skinned body explains
to a contemptuous border officer the need
for Miami's calm, or the Boulevard St Germain's
old-world comforts. Watching the bastards bleed
is tiresome after a bit; you need respite from plastic faces

who beam during the inspirational segment: a blind man
who shits gold, a cripple who makes plastic vases
from Coke bottles, a lisping little girl who can
recite the names of thirty dinosaurs.
        Eight o'clock,
the depression fades, its tears are shed, if their cause
remains a mystery.
    What were the first ideas grokked
by the savages as Columbus and his jackdaws
clambered onto the sand? They might have cried,
to welcome new gods, the leap from stone
to iron, from death by boredom to genocide.
But they wept because they were no longer alone.

11: A MODERN WALDEN

I
And in a flash, it happened, both thinking aloud,
Donald and Jong Un, mocked
into rage, said *What the fuck,*
in unison, and then, cue mushroom cloud.

Apocalypse, the blast, the eerie halo,
the shattering shock wave,
the condo becomes a cave.
But what about the fate of the worlds below —

those sources of spices, vices and refugees?
Those sunny outhouses on sand
serving smiles on demand?
The testing sites for ideologies,

far from Disneyland and the Freedom Tower.
The blast doesn't see borders,
or colonial disorders,
and leaves the wasteland shivering, deflowered.

The lingering afterimage would be haircuts —
Jong Un's pompadour,
Donald's golden shower —
and missiles racing for the era's guts.

II
A band of singed survivors might find, somehow,
a room in the nuclear waste
the blast didn't erase,
and they'd sit bundled at night, soothed by the low

moan and hiss of wind, and squint outside
at the white flakes that slam
the singed spindles of palm
trees, whose crowns had been shorn, water-nuts fried,

but remain upright, a rebellious last stand.
So island borders dissolved,
landscapes have evolved
from wet, leaf-green plains, and cinnamon-sand

to fields of vitrified silica and patches
of stubborn xerophytes,
and new climate blights –
the sun flaying earth in spiteful splashes.

This would be the Walden after the bomb.
The living seek to taste
the marrow of life in haste,
before the radiation sickness can numb

the sharpness in the mouth, and the body's sublime
wholeness, as they wait
for it to degenerate,
measuring the end, beckoning time

to hurry, as now no plots remain to unfold
no fantasy to fill
but Donald and Jong Un's idyll,
to scream into the sky: "*I'm King of the world.*"

12: MODERN EXILE: WELSH LANDSCAPE AT CHRISTMAS
(Found Poem)

We live in a tiny Welsh farming village, high up in the countryside.
Early mornings are so peaceful and beautiful in the winter.
It's always wild at this time in West Wales and yet

we still insist on going for these long walks.
Every walk becomes some sort of crusade.
A long solitary walk has a special grace attached to it as well.

There are views of the surrounding estuaries and fields everywhere.
Our house is on the outskirts, overlooked but not isolated.
I discover exquisite new things all the time.

We live in the old vicarage, so the church is just behind us.
The house is Georgian, old, costs far too much to heat in the winter.
There is wonderful choral music at this time of the year.

Yesterday, there was a wonderful piece by Shostakovich –
first unveiled nine months after Stalin died;
it seems he poured all his repressed emotions into it.

Music like this reflects the words of Akhmatova as well:
The souls of all my dears have flown to the stars,
Thank God there's no one left for me to lose so I can cry.

(Found in emails from Ziska Brown).

13: THE MODERN PARENT

"Will you ever smile again?"
He's stunned at the clarity of this.
She grins, he thinks: *Orthodontist*.
She's precocious; can he explain?

Should he try? And would she get it?
She's asked about cybernetics,
and the meaning of "dialectics"
and said with certainty: "I'd bet

there is no god. It's just a story
people tell themselves to feel
better about the terrible deal
they've got in life. It's kind of gory

when you think about it." How old
was he when he formed the thought?
In what arena had he fought,
at what brutal sport, to be so bold

at age eleven? The school pit,
or home, casual parental abuse –
simple and sick, nothing abstruse?
But his prudish parents never split

and made him into a shuttlecock,
or threw him in to the blood sport
arena of the Family Court,
or put his brain in a headlock

that cost him years, and left him blind
to the sunny magic living in words.
At eight she could not read. The birds
whose songs had calmed his savage mind

Were snared by affidavits and bailiffs.
And his escape, the countryside
Enid Blyton gave children to hide,
was overrun by spiders, motifs

of terror, which frolicked in her head.
Her fairies were Dyslexia,
Asperger's, her bedside text,
The Compendium of Fear and Dread.

It almost broke him; he wishes he could
have taken the lashes, but his own
phoenix had already flown
leaving him marooned in a flood

of missed connections, maddening
misfires, scrambled lines of code
that led him away from the right road
just at the mid-life hardening.

Now, coasting down a different street,
he stares at the wide, furrowed forehead,
the rebellious curls, the red
sliver between the rabbit teeth.

And he thinks, as he answers slowly,
Look at this wonder I've helped create:
her mother's face, her father's innate
restless temperament: the holy

relics of a happier state.
"Why not say something funny and see?"
The brow and jaw stiffen and she
sighs and figures how long she'll wait

before he concedes she knows about lies,
and they have no purchase in the vast
vista she sees, one where the past
he hides struggles a little, then dies.

14: MODERN MYTH: A SINGLE TRANSLATION OF TWO POEMS
(for Caryl Phillips)

(i) *Ekalavya*
(A fragment of the *Mahabharata*)

Today they'd say "minority", or "child
of nature", but an age ago, in the Kuru empire
he was *Nishada*, an aristocrat of the wild,

who rose as a yuga spun in a dying gyre,
when, to crown the Pandavas in Bharat, the Deva
court plotted a gory epic of death by fire.

Just a bit player, was brave Ekalavya,
who'd studied Stanislavski – *there are no small
parts...* and the hero isn't always the saviour.

And outcaste or no, his heart leapt at the call
of conch shells, of blood throbbing in temples
and the hiss of arrows, screaming as they fall.

Ambition aside, it is courage that often resembles
fate, and the wildling sought as *acharya* and master,
Drona, the Brahman who schooled the assembled

princes in war and death-craft for the disaster
spectacle in the making – both hero and foil,
Durodyhana and Arjuna, and a cast

of hundreds – brothers, cousins, blood and soil.
Ekalavya reverently approached the Brahman
and was rejected; inside the mortal coil,

(ii) *Caliban*
(A fragment of *The Tempest*)

They told him later his mother was Sycorax,
a witch, when they saw none of their attacks

could pierce or break his miraculous dark skin –
axe-heads broke, lead shot crumpled like tin –

and conventional war now useless, they thought they'd find
an unguarded flank in his gullible savage mind.

In Africa, she'd poisoned the biblical nations,
corrupted the old Pharaonic civilisations,

she'd taunted their old men, who seethed in silence
and scoured the parchments for suitable violence

to inflict upon her. They found an ancient spell
to turn the word to life, and cast it to dwell

inside her, and, weakened as the child began
to grow in the form of a misshapen man,

the old men combined their might and hurled
her across an ocean, to the void of a new world,

where she gave birth to him in a fertile valley
and named him after her godmother, Kali.

And thus, for Caliban's sake, she waged a war
to establish his rights under ancient law.

Its logic was simple and brutal: the spoils belong
to the most vicious and their allies: the strong.

rules of caste forbade. Crestfallen, he calmly
asked a blessing, which Drona absently spoke,
and released him, waving a pale, callused palm.

But martial ambition is roiling, restless. He woke
every morning with Drona's face burning
in his savage mind, and in the entrails of smoke

he saw a way. To create, he must first return
to primal mud, the source of all things. He kneeled
and dug his fingers into the dirt, and relearned

the mysteries of the low castes who grease the wheel
of life. From the sacred earth all things had come
and in its atoms were memories. He could feel

the points and ridges of forgotten wisdom
inscribing lines on the palms buried in mud,
etching the route to the walled-off kingdom.

He moulded a mud statue of Drona, his god;
lovingly aligning the proud nose and chin,
smoothing the Brahman skin, and the blue blood

he imagined running beneath, untouched by sin
or inane desire – like lust, revenge, ambition.
This was Drona, as Drona should have been.

And eyeing his preceptor, of his own volition
the wildling derived the poetics of the bow,
and perfected it. Arrows inscribed his mission

in the hearts of muscular stems, through the flow
of forest streams to impale furtive eels,
the silver mail of the carp, the flattened brow

The local gods were naïve, could not withstand
the maelstrom of germs and steel at her command.

To bind the primitives with shock and awe
she locked Ariel, their god, in a pine core,

and seeing their Zemi defeated with such ease
the Tainos dissipated into the breeze.

He remembered tapering fingers, an ochre hand
tracing mystical seals in the white sand

to bind the elements, the streams, the beasts
while incanting: *Cali, you must be free of priests*.

So by the time Prospero and his daughter
arrived, the land knew him alone; his laughter

woke up the birds and enraged the flitting sprites
who, to escape, surrendered the days for nights.

But his magic, never having to face a foe,
was overwhelmed by the practised Prospero.

His mother's law, the Magus said, applied:
in defeat, the weaker should submit and abide,

as he freed Ariel from his wooden cage
and showed him to Caliban as his alter-image.

The conquered Caliban became a trusty,
and carried wood and water, mindful of the rusty

collar that hung around his veiny neck,
which tightened at Prospero's airy beck.

of the magur. The years passed; the yugas' wheels
spun as prescribed, and finally, Drona
was drawn into his orbit. His princes' heels

were hot to escape training targets' stony
faces. They desired prey, the spoor of dread
and grunts of fear to foreshadow the death moans

of the coming war, and its legions of red-eyed dead.
At the head of the royal train, at Drona's side
sat Arjuna, wielder of the Gandiva, his head

in Indra's crown, and carried by the tide
of legend, myth, and unpredictable fate.
The caravan, of creaking howdahs astride

bleary elephants, cavalry, guides waiting
on hounds to point the archers to game,
abruptly stopped, as beasts were startled at a spate

of muffled screams from a bloody bitch who came
to sight and hearing. Her muzzle was pierced with five
arrows from five angles, a suture to tame

the bitch's deadliest weapon – her mouth. The caravan
stops and Drona descended to inspect
the uncanny marksman's art. *No one in heaven,*

or earth, not Arjuna, could achieve this perfection,
This is an illusion, a Rakshasa
or Deva is sporting here. Let us direct

Our train elsewhere. As Arjuna nodded, a flash
of white enamel broke the green-sleeved branches
and Ekalavya strode to Drona, unabashed

But Caliban never ceased to listen and dream.
His mother's magic still ran in his blood stream

to comfort the raging mind in the malformed body,
and Caliban flourished as the Magus's understudy:

combining his white magic with Sycorax's dark,
he began to see the fire in the spark;

that single droplets became the fearsome flood;
that every powerful race began in mud.

And Caliban foresaw a time would come
when the Magus would fade, leaving him his freedom,

and the greatest law of conquest was fickle fate,
who decreed the wisest strategy was to wait.

He spoke with Prospero and learned the logic
that drove the conqueror's white magic.

He listened to the magician's unguarded words
when he sat alone, confiding in the birds,

and learned the nuance in weight and tone, the spaces
in between that revealed the language's secret places.

He combined the diction used with him, and the softer
words that passed between Prospero and his daughter.

Thus Caliban's lexis began to grow and change
as feeling found meaning. Now watching him, a strange

admiration grew in Prospero
for the genius of lonely anti-hero.

by bristling Kshatriyas raising jewelled ganches
and laid himself prostrate at the Brahman's feet –
the posture of student to master – and Arjuna blanches

as the realisation of the lesser meeting
the greater took hold. He turns in surprise,
then rage to his master, who returns the greeting:

*But who are you, young warrior? Rise,
and speak*. A shy smile splits the wildling face,
and Ekalavya spoke, and lovingly reprises

the first encounter, rejection, the request for grace
in the blessing, his sculpting Drona's image,
which now resided in his holiest place.

As he listens, Drona feels the rippling rage
in Arjuna's heart. Divinity dethroned
by instinct and genius without lineage.

An age and heaven's mechanics grates in Drona
as he weighed divine right against Sudra sweat.
He turns to the Nishada: *My son, you have grown*

past my expectation. But you owe a debt:
A guru must have his dakshina *for the pact
to be complete*. The Nishada's face set

in reverence and he says: *If I lack
this, Master, I am bound to pay. Just name
the fee you desire.* And the ruthless Drona attacks:

I demand the thumb of your right hand. The blameless
Nishada laughs with joy and addresses his master:
I give it gladly, like clarified butter to flame.

But Caliban never ceased to listen and dream.
His mother's magic still ran in his blood stream

to comfort the mind in his malformed, brutish body,
and Caliban flourished as Prospero's understudy:

combining his white magic with Sycorax's dark,
he began to see the fire in the spark;

that single droplets became the fearsome flood;
that every powerful race began in mud.

And Caliban foresaw a time would come
when the Magus would fade, leaving him his freedom,

and the greatest law of conquest was fickle fate,
who decreed the wisest strategy was to wait.

He spoke with Prospero and learned the logic
that drove the conqueror's white magic.

He listened to the magician's unguarded words
when he sat alone, confiding in the birds,

and learned the nuance in weight and tone, the spaces
in between that revealed the language's secret places.

He combined the diction used with him, and the softer
words that passed between Prospero and his daughter.

And Caliban's lexis began to grow and change
as feeling found meaning. Now watching him, a strange

admiration grew in Prospero
for the genius of lonely anti-hero

His laughter is rich and real, and casts a
halo around him as he departs. He might
have laughed at the Devas, who'd amassed

an army of semi-divines, and myths of their plight,
to retell an ancient drama, whose climax was war,
and whose moral remained the virtue of divine right.

He might have wondered at the other flaws
in divine logic, and other atrocities
that lived as virtue in caste and karmic laws.

But Ekalavya fades quietly;
he knows for dying animals, chained to life,
war is the answer to pious sobriety.

and his tenacity to invent, then move,
the bricks of language he needed to disprove

the conqueror's rights on the single ground of force.
But fate had set events, and a ship, on course

to the far island, and in the drama that followed
Caliban found that words could also be hollow.

Every man desired the same irrational thing —
to be restored to his rightful place as king,

and Prospero was no different: he carried
the reverence for royalty, and wished to marry

his daughter to it, and to live in its affliction
and scheme against his eventual eviction.

With his mind raging at the thought of reparation,
Prospero thought of Caliban's station:

*Let him remain a servant; the frontier needs
a brute; to allow a slave to think and reason feeds*

*the beast of revenge. To manumit too soon's
just folly*. And left him at the mercy of drunken buffoons,

Stephano and Trinculo, his regents
who became the legislators and travel agents

for the Middle Passage package tour to attract
souls to fill the void left by Sycorax.

But first, they waged a new war on her son;
only with his defeat could the land be won.

The campaign changed when tools of conventional war
could not reach his malleable core,

and unable to breach the stony body's defences,
they aimed the spectral weapons at his subtle senses.

Unable to attack him, they went for his mother:
Look, the breast that fed you poisoned another.

Caliban, reflecting on it all, could see
the strategy, and discovered irony.

Not genius, nor bravery, nor guile
could drive the headwaters of the Nile;

the builder of the pyramids, the Pharaoh,
married his sister because, like Prospero,

he did not know or trust the world's design,
which had revealed itself in Caliban's mind.

15: MODERN DEATH: FRANNIE AND JIMMY ARE DEAD
(A screenplay)

J: So, Franz, you look the same as yesterday.
 Your face remains uncreased by drink or laughter,
 you wear the same gloomy coat and vest, so grey
 in this bright place.

K: As you know, J, I prefer
 to be called K. And I see nothing here that makes
 me feel differently. This place does not differ
 from the last one. The seraphim are too bright
 and this mist — what's beneath it? You are too
 gullible, J…

J: Come, Franz, doesn't the sight
 of all this heraldry move you to tears? The singing,
 flowers, manifestations of desires…

K: Light. Song. How simple you are. The only thing
 I wanted was nothingness.

J: Perhaps, old man,
 It's not your wants that matter here, the game
 is not so simple as you might think. The plan
 behind all this might yet elude you.

K: But if
 there is some other design, who controls
 it? And why am I here not knowing? What if
 whoever draws the design is not concerned
 with our wisdom, but their own amusement?

J: You've forgotten pleasure, my friend. I've earned
 some respite from age and blindness, and from the looks
 on my daughter's face, and Nora's; all appears
 as perfect as cream — and they like my books.

K: I left those earthly attachments behind. Max
was charged with strict instructions, which he ignored.
But still, it's not my concern now. This lacks
not only explanation, but purpose, as far
as I can tell.

J: You are so stubborn.
Don't you want to see your father? He's here,
you know, waiting for you. And your mother.
Perhaps you're here not for your benefit
but theirs.

K: My father... Here? No, another
useless exculpation. I have no wish
to see him. As for my mother, she made her choice;
...but, wait, if this is the place you insist...

What about truth? Your daughter is here, sane
and loving you, your daughter you drove mad...
no, J, any place that relieves our pain
unconditionally must be fiction.

J: And what in the universe is not fiction?
As long as we're allowed choice, why not pick one
that gives us even illusory joy? Would you
prefer illusory pain?

K: I want illusions undone –
the lie of justice to start; isn't it true
that joy fades as pain endures? A moment of joy
is just that. But an instant of pain echoes.

J: You were a very unhappy little boy
weren't you? By quibbling, all you
do is delay the infinite...

K: This is tiresome.
    What good is life if any novel could brew
    the same confusions and happy accidents,
    into inane redemption? What profit
    is there in seeing a life through some lens
    of false meaning?

J: You defeat yourself, Franz,
    before the game's begun. Perhaps there is
    no end. Perhaps it's an infinite card game, with hands
    endlessly following hands. Why not
    sit and play a while? Oh, you have the time,
    time seems to be most abundant here, a glut
    almost. I know we've met before, but still,
    each time I see you, it's as if we're meeting anew.

(*K sits down and allows J to deal him some cards*)

K: Yes, yes. An infinite card game. But what will
    we play for? It must be something of value
    or why bother? Now don't you agree, J?

J: For once you're right, Frannie. Now what would do
    for currency if everything we want
    is provided as we wish it?

K: What about
    a freedom from illusion? You recant
    a cherished belief everytime I win…

J: And what about the times you lose?

K: Ah, then
    I follow you, commit your choice of sin.

J: And what if, in the end, one has relieved

    the other of his burden completely? If
    at the close, you unshakably believed
    in my fantasies, or I was made bereft
    and saw the world in grey like you. What would
    the other do? I mean, what fun would be left?

K: The answer is simple, J. Each one loses
    what he gives the other. So, if one's filled
    with joy and one empty, the joyful one poses
    the same argument you posed to me, and
    the game begins again.

J: That sounds familiar,
    Franz, though how, I can't fully understand;
    it's almost like a fiction.

K: And what is there
    in the universe that is not a fiction?

AGE, &C.

16: BIRTHDAY BOY

It doesn't occur to him to resist the urge,
so he looks back through time, and sighs at the sight.
The moment isn't morbid enough for a dirge
or dreadful metaphors of encroaching night.
The morning is bland; he is alone; the apartment
glares back at him, ready for anything.
He fumbles, stumbles, and mumbles a smart comment
he should have made – about his wearing an earring –
twenty-five years ago, talking to someone
who probably owns a home, and goes to Rotary
meetings now. *Is that how he should've gone?*
He mulls the alternate timeline: a notary
public? A votary in an obscure religion
whose sacraments are Coke and cake for breakfast?

The caffeine slaps him; the sugar tints his vision;
and braced and deceived, he rummages the bleak past
and settles into the marsupial pouch of the sofa,
and bids the inevitable to proceed.

*Is YouTube on the television too far
along the road to decadence?* The speed
is picking up, and fate is flinging hints
he's happy to ignore, but does consider
the day auspicious enough for music: Prince
And George Michael: the rebel outsider,
the beautiful toff; both dead this awful year,
but leaving their songs. He sits entranced as The Kid
intones the blessing, then proceeds to tear
into *Let's Go Crazy*, which, he recalls, undid
in him a knot of terrible childhood fear.
As the final silky shriek expires, the crisper
arrangements of *Wham!* follow: George, the careful
androgyny, the earrings, and *Careless Whisper.*

The autoplay kicks in, offers The Isley Brothers,
Teena Marie, Annie Lennox, and he sinks
gratefully into the private vortex, which smothers
the thoughts that burble, and eventually, it shrinks
and dissipates, leaving him where he started:
in his birthday suit, ashamed at having cried
at OMD's "If You Leave", and brokenhearted
because he knows the world is waiting outside.

17: THE APPROACH

I will be here, always, for you
always; time will not undo

the knot of gold and mercury
that binds our hearts' rhyming fury...

Overheard on television,
in throes of passion or derision –

you don't hear it like that any more
outside a BD dungeon's door.

Why have tongues become so thrifty,
just because we approach fifty?

When eternity is so much closer
and deceit, that slippery old poser,

now an ally, not the flaneur
we chased away when time was not so clear?

It's hard to do anything but panic,
after trusting dodgy, manic

fate to resolve nervy chaos
of fickle fault lines, that cross

borders into a magical world
with no thought for immigration control.

I suppose some lucky sprites
slipped through on moonlit nights

but the rest of us, with misfiring tricks,
remain prisoners of the norm: statistics.

And years later, unable to forget,
thanks to the fucking Internet,

we sprawl behind island blinds
scrying impossible time-lines

unfolding on YouTube or Netflix,
as we slide helplessly down the Styx.

18: MIDWAY

It's sudden: you find, one day,
the jokes no longer funny;
in shock you wonder if they
ever were, and smile at the bunny

in the slut dress and sneakers,
the Instagram lips and hair,
as the riffs crash like breakers
on a smooth cliff, the career

adrift not far behind.
Irony hoists a sail:
So much for the life of the mind.
But it's not the mind that failed.

Nothing's amiss; it's just fifty.
The familiar road's worn out.
Even on land, you drift,
unable to come about,

or find your way in terrain
you'd thought already mapped,
its topoi wired in the brain,
whose folds can't be unwrapped.

II

Fifty sounds like midway,
but to where? The past appears
to not have led to today:
a time machine whose gears

have spun your faith into chaos.
A set of loose-knit dreams
whose random plotlines cross
like bursting, nervy streams.

Could it all be as banal
as nature? We're meant to die,
but not everyone gets a finale
beneath a sheltering sky.

Maybe it's just the bunny,
your tired, fleshy face,
the price of irony:
you're an acquired taste.

You're in a different time
and you're down on your luck;
your destiny seems to mime
the self-effacing Prufrock,

who saw himself at sea,
but on its lonely floors
treading aimlessly
on hopeless, ragged claws.

19: FROM 30 TO T2

At thirty I was flirty, besotted
with the snarky anarchy of *Trainspotting*.

I loved the speed of Renton's run,
the face alight like a white sun,

a red-eyed demon, skimming past
the shop windows' sclerotic glass.

He escaped, got away with it
and embraced life, or something like it:

A wife in Amsterdam, a job,
Amstel Light for the gaping gob.

Then it all went away, thanks to
Schumpeter, the funds, the banks;

"creative destruction", the final words
you hear as they flush human turds,

and financiers playing musical chairs
mulct billions from human fears.

But that is nature: capitalism
feeding on youthful nihilism,

and after 20 years, Renton
understood just what went on.

It all turned shitty as they'd expected;
he regretted having genuflected

to the television dream and drunk
the promise of life without the junk.

He should've stayed high, on the dole,
like Spud, who stayed in the rabbit hole,

or Sick Boy, faithful to his core:
blackmail, a bar, the personable whore.

But he left, driven by propaganda,
to a world about to be pulled asunder

by what Begbie called fookin' cunts,
also known as bankers and quants,

and after 20 years awoke
to sounds of alarum and smelling smoke.

It was all coming apart, the city
was being sacked without pity,

but not by bearded, turbaned hordes;
the looters were pin-striped corporate boards.

So he packed his bundle as the wrecker
arrived, and trundled back to his Mecca.

He calculated his amends –
the price of betraying old friends –

paid it, took the punches and sneers
and made his way to the foot of the stairs,

and ascended to die in his old room,
dancing his way to grinning doom.

Sick Boy's regressed to being a louse;
Begbie is back in the big house.

Because at fifty, we understand,
if there is a plan, it isn't grand.

20: LETTER TO 25.

I remember you were a budding cynic
back then, so hear the bad news first:
the angry sky wasn't just scenic;
the rain persists as the noose of thirst

tightens. Kind of like Howard Jones
crooning: *You can feel the cushion,
but you can't have a seat* – it's agones
and strife; brutish, empty of passion.

This wasn't the plan, or your chosen part.
You wanted to keep it honest, mostly,
and sue for decency. The smart
money would win in time; the gross

matter transmuted to fine metal,
ductile enough to stitch the flayed
body. And the theme-song you settled
on – the sappy romantic ballad: Sinead

O'Connor's *Nothing Compares to You*,
written by Prince – who you were quite
smitten by, and never outgrew.
Now Prince has gone to the good night,

with Larry Durrell and Joseph K –
your antipodes – hope and irony,
who warred with the implacable grey
polity of the penal colony,

sure that meaning would be at the gate
of Chapel Perilous and yield
to the knight errant, not the ingrate
lawyer's clerk, or intern, or congealed

muck of ambition and lust kneaded
to a man-shape. But you were wrong.
The hollow men's amorphous creed,
their feckless greed, were what the strong

needed most: automata
for the new world they were dreaming,
a place where the only virtue is data
and its virtual angels, vice and scheming.

Yes, the world's become something different
from what you'd hoped: its flowers are metal;
its ichor of zeroes and ones is spent
on vice; its mind cannot settle.

Amidst it all you float, an island
almost, that remains undiscovered.
Its overgrown temples and steles are grand,
its beaches blank, awaiting lovers.

It's a lonely state, the imagination,
but I live there still, in these later days
along with a reminder of salvation,
a moody metonym with a ticklish gaze –

I mean our daughter, who lives with me
but no wife. And I don't want to take
the story off course, on a flight of fancy
too distant, with leaps impossible to make

between your present and your future.
And I'd leave out the finest part
of you, which healed the ancient rupture
in a dying animal's beastly heart.

The heart. I have so far been silent
on love, as a means or an end. And here
my younger knight, the most violent
upset awaits: the truth laid bare.

It's an illusion, tricks of chemistry,
whose sprites and sirens will tease
and twist, and whisper mystery
to no end. It's just a beautiful beast

without purpose, whose flesh we tasted
and were entranced. Some men know this;
we do not, somehow, and caution is wasted
to tell us. And I want you to persist

in this foolish quest, self-doubting knight,
because it leads you to me. This isn't defeat.
between us, we're not drained of fight:
we live the joy of dying on our feet.

21: AN IMPERFECT ENDING

I
A blue breathing tube filled your trachea.
Your eldest son, half-dreaming it would wake you,
whispered the sacred "Om" in your wooden ears.

But you heard only the Bollywood refrain
rippling along the folds of your tremulous brain
as its restive crackling slowed in the bone coffin.

II
Your horoscope predicted a life of misfortune
but was silent on death, on a Sunday afternoon
after your sons had gone, and you lay alone.

The sterile scent, the icy hospital smock,
the hoses, the accordion lung: your death gasp mocked
your life, as science diffused havan smoke.

III
In the days that followed each of the six sons
would wake in the pre-dawn, with trembling hands
scribbling messages on your list of demands:

the ritual, the cloves, the alignment of the bier.
Each would do as bid and, as each prayer
echoed, carom between relief and grief.

IV
The oldest son would dream, on Mother's Day,
of you in another house, and in old clothes,
on the transom, in a familiar pose.

In that moment, fifty years will fly,
his eyes will close, his throat will wring itself tight
and utter his first cry: *You are my light.*

V
Your sons will laugh and carry the pine box,
they'll remember your endless wishing for this,
and pray there is no samsara for you, just bliss.

But the goddesses of Devaloka have eyes
only for Kardashians. The skies
are blank, without feeling, as your pyre blazes.

22: TWO ELEGIES

(i) *The Monk and the Buddha*

I
You might protest I'm not the fittest poet
for this; I was closest to you, like a young Auden
adoring Byron, but you chose to never know it.
(Conceited, yes, but better irreverent than maudlin.)

And in the spirit of the rebellious monk
paddling in the Buddha's wake, or a whore,
I'll admit it's posterity, that gorgeous drunk,
not regret, that calls me to write your story.

It echoes Lowell and Bishop guiding you,
your bringing me to the firm: and I stayed with it,
and your coda: *Study the masters, make it new.*
Avoid vers libre, *there's always a meter to fit it.*

But now, the tireless hammer of craft has stopped
beating, and the old firm's been slowly bled
by fledglings born in liberal ledgers and sopped
with white guilt, demanding to be drunk and fed.

The trade has changed and nowadays it's packed
with truculent hacks, hired for reasons other
than talent, or love of learning – more the knack
for bleating. It's money, and multi-culti, that smothered

the word, as Vidia might say; the revenge of the prigs
sold as self-esteem, or equality,
but it's just vice, as subtle as Circe's pigs.
Now, verse is mood, and art, velleity.

You railed against this kind of thing an age
ago — *Illiteracy must be recognised
for what it is: a defect* — from your stage
in Trinidad, which you saw as hell in disguise.

II
I've lived in Hades for half a century;
our lives don't parallel, but sometimes rhyme;
I couldn't afford bohemian penury
and had to fight my way to the fading sublime.

But I traced your path, and took a seat on the board
of your first company, and watched it wobble
on oblivion's lip for a decade, mourning its lord.
In the end, nostalgia wasn't worth the trouble.

(And I know why you left; I read the letter
and heard the testimony, which was appalling,
and really, to leave in anger was the better
choice — as was dying, before #Me Too came calling.)

And then the *Guardian*, arena for epic fights
with Errol Hill, the flaying of phony artists,
the selfie interviews, the libels, the slights —
your victims were legion, and though not the smartest

they could have taught you something about survival.
The artists manqué you mangled remain breathing,
and they're still trying to pimp the Carnival
as ersatz art, and racial rage's still seething.

You learned history was a nightmare we dreamed
from Joyce and Vico. I looked to Kubrick instead.
Whatever our sins, primates are only redeemed
by fighting to death with femurs of our dead.

III
In other places, the geist is not so dark
as in Trinidad. But those born with its stamp
are haunted by its stinging, indelible mark –
and like leery Vidia, choose the early decamp.

But there's still light in your exchanges with him.
Even the *Guardian's* jaundiced pages show,
as the newsprint and sepia photos go dim,
the marvellous fruit our barren trees can grow.

His early success piqued; you worked in the dark,
he sat in the liberal lap and hectored new nations
as you wrote them songs and moral fables to mark
their births. But in the end they were empty oblations;

the twilight spoke, and you knew he was right.
The dreadful end was written in the beginning,
and revolutions descended to racial spite,
the oldest battle they'd fantasised winning.

So, near the end, it was awful that you'd choose
to sit with the new "Caribbean" culturati,
accuse and lynch the enigmatic Mongoose,
and revive the revolutionary party

you once despised. And when you left, they cursed
your divided vein by turning on the "white"
Caribbean writers, as their forebears cut Perse
and seized Césaire to press the majority's right.

It's Joyce's nightmare all over again: repeating
history. You dreamed a new Aegean in bloom
in these islands, from old civilisations' meeting.
But some flowers are born to blush unseen in a tomb.

(ii) *The Lark of Darkness*

I.
In the streets in Port of Spain the steel bands fumble
and grope for notes. A bassman shakes his head.
The milling crowds, restless, begin to grumble
and fidget. A fugue stirs: *Look, Naipaul dead*.

Of course they did nothing of the kind, Vidia;
Brahmanic disdain still draws the blackest looks
in this Republic of the Bottom Feeder
where they hate you, but cannot read your books.

But they belong in your last poem, because here
is where you began, it's where you kept returning:
to the strange nation born of original fear
where, somehow, Promethean fire keeps burning.

But they would not see Prometheus; it was Biswas
they would tolerate, the hero in disguise;
their mythos needed a Blaxploitation badass,
whose antagonist they could safely despise.

And they still haven't got over the shock;
Shaft was their hero, known for poisonous pique.
He treated them with disdain, but was their rock,
and when he barked, no damned dog dared speak.

You were Yul Brynner, riding into the sunset,
sardonic, inscrutable, on a dark horse;
they couldn't bear it, and they couldn't forget
the style which matadored their ox-like force.

And still the nationalists nurture petty rage,
cursing *The Middle Passage* and *Mimic Men*.
Your death, a pierced moment on the big stage,
barely registered in the land of the Douen.

(But on that Sunday, irony stormed the stage.
In Chaguanas, where you were born, pink apes stripped
a woman of her yellow sari; the image
echoed, and the government said, through thick, red lips

*It's all in fun, it's just a skit, you're being
paranoid. It was our Family Day.
Don't believe it's Fanonian sickness you're seeing,
this isn't a prelude, it's just guerillas at play.)*

It's ended as you said in confusion;
they live in terror that just won't go away;
they shield themselves with violent illusion.
One word remains: *Santimanitay*.

II.
If there's a place after this woeful world
you've found a club up there, with a reading room,
chintzy armchairs to recline, compose, and unfold
the *Spectator*, with conversations in bloom.

Was this the sort of thing you despised or yearned?
You weren't a pleasant man from beginning to end,
but neither were those you pursued, used, then spurned.
You shared this picaroon trait with the other Caribbean

rake — your doppelganger and twin — *Shabine*
he might want to be called, or just Derek.
It was that essential island instinct, rapine,
that let you build a castle from a shipwreck.

You each had what the other lacked. You marvelled
at his ease among the Blacks, and their worship.
Unable to be alone, he watched you revel
in lonely strife, and taunt the liberal whip,

laughingly dropping tales of beating whores,
as he sought fraternity in a phony exile,
and draped a stony silence to cover his sores.
He modelled Don Juan on your shy, thin-lipped smile

as you modelled your gaze on Conrad's restless eye,
and Froude's relentless logic. Every man
is a monarch; equality is our comforting lie;
and every monarchy is built on sand.

III.
I imagine the afterlife club is lively on evenings
as gin-hoarse voices sing and cigar smoke thickens,
and the tail-coated butlers wheel out the leavings
waiting for the fashionably late Dickens.

The names you recited, like a list of vices –
Powell, Joyce and Hazlitt, and Waugh (who once
said it was your dark face that won your prizes) –
are there, and strutting around like Oxford dons.

In time you'll see it's all an egoist charade.
The bodies will become seraphs, and bow to greet
the haloed imago: Seepersad,
as you complete your circle, at his feet.

23: THE DIVINE BODY AT PRAYER
(For Alicia Lewis)

How does that body set itself to pray?
How do the coltish legs inflect at the knee?
How does the trilling voice soften to say
the Angelus? And does the filigree
of delicate cilia running along the Grecian
neck tremble at the promise of a hollow blessing?
And what about the wondrous nexus, the junction
where spine and waist meet, and where the dress
creases as the fabric drapes the slope
of unthinkable parts, that do not face the altar,
but tilt irresistibly toward the world,
outside the grace of the sacrament you curl
into your tongue, where it rests like a star
whose brightness delights lonely pagan hope?

*

A pagan would be appalled seeing your body
kneeling in prayer. He would think it perverse – tragic
if his savage mind could rise out of its muddy
state, and conceive the horror of churchly magic.
He might think of a deer, or a swan, in its place
in the order of things; the savagery of forcing
those limbs to bend to adore a marble face
whose eyes are blind, and the only thing coursing
through its veins is dogma. The savage would see
a different enchantment limning those velvet limbs
and wonder at the virtue which despises distaff,
that chains a spirit, and grows as its light dims.
And he would wonder, looking at that bent knee,
whether the god allowed the mouth to laugh.

24: THE UNFINISHED

An unfinished poem is a dreary thing.
It's not a statue with a missing limb,
unripened fruit, a crow with a white wing.
It has no charm. It sits, unsmiling, grim,
waiting to slip from nothing into existence.
Like Schrodinger's Cat, it sprawls between two states
whose relations are historically tense;
embroiled in skirmishes, wars, political debates
to settle the seething question: *Do I exist?*
In this the poem's a golem of its maker:
a tout, who slinks amidst reality's alleys
and theatres, seeking patterns in chaos, the mist
of careless utterance, from prophet and faker,
to harness them with words to drive his sallies.

*

An unfinished novel is a kind of animal –
forlorn, in incompletion; its scenes and heroes
haunt the mind of its maker. It is a cannibal
stalking reality, like a biro's
ball gobbles ink, a lion devours a Christian.
The novel's themes and social agenda
take on bodies; they scream and piss on
their maker, like a parson on a bender.
It's because the novel is a life, designed
to fight to live, to confront every danger,
unlike a poem, which is a feckless angel
unconcerned with the tortured human mind.
Its domain is the misty, the ethereal, the stranger
vaults of the heart, where hope still lives in a manger.

25: THE STARSHIP *ENTERPRISE*

Einstein could saddle a wild beam of light
and roam the starry trails of the universe.
The rest of us just look into the night
and float in the mute longing to immerse
constricting memory, skin, and viscera
into the velvet beyond the fantasies
of dewy pudenda, food, and denatured terror –
the malaise of the sick, released from earthly disease.

*

Astronauts yearning for interstellar travel
are dreaming of death. The distance between shores
crosses lifetimes. In space, their bodies unravel.
Without gravity, the fundamental laws
fail. The vertebrae loosen and separate.
The molecules dissociate and release
errant ions to float along the strait
between organs like ronin, or heretic priests.

*

The desire to stand on a starship's bridge and watch
in awe is the first religion: not to master
the majesty outside, but to detach
from infinity, which roars as it rushes past.
The monad, insulated, self-contained,
sleeps inside the Magellanic Cloud
among pulsing stars, dreaming of a domain
of ribcages, burning eyes, and heads unbowed.

26: UNREQUITED: TO A COY SPINSTER

I know too well, my tortured dear,
The spiky root of this paralysing fear

that pulls you to my eccentric orbit,
then drives you back into the straight and morbid.

Your life on the bourgeois asteroid
that spun for decades in the starless void

has taught you love is depravity,
and you foolishly fear its gentle gravity.

Vanity sends you to retreat
and covers your defeat with grey conceit.

And there's the source of your pretty pain –
your deepest wounds are dreadfully mundane –

the hurt, the parents, and all that slop –
it's tame; as Larkin said, *They fuck you up.*

They do it to us all, from the proles
to the loftiest of liberated souls,

and what we do is take it and grin
and accept that here, the wounded cannot win.

Like you, the world is fickle and flawed
and enlightenment often comes via two-by-four,

and life won't yield unless you spur it
with commands from the mouth of a pushy poet,

who doesn't know restraint or patience
and only answers to Romantic conscience.

So darling, make me your two-by-four,
and I'll scratch along my unpolished length: *I adore*

the Neurotic, forty-something Siren,
with instincts frozen by faulty island wiring.

And if I can't be your two-by-four,
I'll be the gentle knocking on your door –

the jolt that helps you realize
the speed at which time's wingèd chariot flies.

You'd see a different world, my dear,
if joy, not time, would crack the sulky veneer.

27: AN ISLAND IN THE SEA

When rain and wind savage the surface
the deep is quite a different place.
Lying on the floor, looking upwards,
you see the watery splinters and shards
that rise in rage, then scream and explode,
replaying a vital episode
of the dramas of the depths unfurled
against the ceiling of the world.

*

The surface colours change with seasons:
the blue and green, and oily lesions,
the dirty brown and sickly yellows
that deltas and river mouth bellows
breathe out in bursts of pregnant flood,
to provide an inscribed layer of mud
from terra's grip, in a water casement,
to archive in the ocean's basement.

*

Below the surface, just one colour
persists: blue, which fades to dolour.
The oceanic state led Freud
to dive into the abyss that buoyed
the fragile sun-seeking ego,
to explore the deepest drives of indigo
depths, and the denser medium than air
that nurtures original, tameless fear.

*

To live on an island, surrounded by sea
is to live remorseless irony.
The island is a fragile state
anchored in deeper forces that wait
for cues from unseen legislators,
to be moved about by moody curators.
All island lives are coloured by fear
of Leviathans from the depths of despair.

ABOUT THE AUTHOR

Raymond Ramcharitar was born in Trinidad. He worked as a journalist and is the author of a controversial and provocative study of the deficiencies of the Trinidadian press, Breaking the News: Media & Culture in Trinidad. He is the author of two previous collections of poetry, *American Fall* and *Here,* and a collection of short stories, *The Island Quintet: Five Stories*.

ALSO BY RAYMOND RAMCHARITAR

American Fall
ISBN: 9781845230432; pp. 72; pub. 2007; £7.99

Raymond Ramcharitar's sophisticated and formally ambitious poems have Trinidad as their centre but are global in scope. This is reflected both in their subject matter and their form. The regular movement between the Caribbean, Europe and North America that several of the poems chart is seen both as a contemporary reality, and as no more than a continuation of history's patterns: of, for instance, Indo-Trinidadians who are the 'scions of waylaid Brahmins and pariahs'.

This particular migration is placed in the context of a wider world of human movement and 'new theologies springing from old longings'. In form, too, the poems refuse to be confined by any limiting sense of the contemporary and the Caribbean. Use of the archetypes of classical mythology, traditional verse patterns (such as the villanelle) and the careful, confident use of rhythm and rhyme are the most evident outward features of Ramcharitar's concern with form. There are homages to Derek Walcott and Wallace Stevens, but the closer one's acquaintance with the poems, the more evident that Ramcharitar's post-modern voice is a thoroughly individual one, with a capacity for writing verse narratives that are condensed but reverberate like the best short stories, dramatic monologues that skilfully create other voices, and lyric poems that get inside the less obvious byways of emotion.

Here
ISBN: 9781845232122; pp. 72; pub. 2013; £8.99

Here is a book-length autobiographical poem in five parts, addressing the large themes of the Caribbean experience: history, migration, myth, and domestic love.

Here marks the first poetic approach to re-visioning and recreating Caribbean mythology on an epic scale, which remains dominated by Kamau Brathwaite's *Arrivants* and Derek Walcott's *Another Life*.

The different movements of *Here* vary in style and tone (from blank verse, to terza rima, to heroic couplets), but are unified by the voice of the single narrator, which changes over time. *Here* is prefaced by a passage from the *Ramayana* and the poem begins on the plains of Caroni, where the narrator traces his beginnings.

From this start, the poem moves to an overnight bus journey through Europe, a sojourn in Toronto, and an account of a broken marriage, addressed to the narrator's daughter. The series of poems ends with 'The Last Avatar', a mini-epic which re-casts the Caribbean as a Hindu eschatological myth, and places its heroes as the holy trinity, of Brahma, Shiva and Vishnu in Caribbean terms.

"The intelligence and formal skill of Raymond Ramcharitar embodies what Wallace Stevens meant when he said that the poetry we value most proclaims/ The near, the clear while also giving back to us the the imagination that we spurned and crave." Tom Sleigh.

The Island Quintet
ISBN: 9781845230753; pp. 232; pub. 2009; £8.99

Raymond Ramcharitar's vision is rooted in Trinidad, but as a globalised island with permeable borders, frequent birds of passage, and outposts in New York and London. One of the collection's outstanding qualities is that it is both utterly contemporary and written with a profound and disturbed sense of the history that shapes the island.

As befits fiction from the home of carnival and mas', it is a collection much concerned with the flesh – often in transgressive forms as if characters are driven to test their boundaries – and with the capacity of its characters to reinvent themselves in manifold, and sometimes outrageous disguises. One of the masks is race, and the stories are acerbically honest about the way tribal loyalties distort human relations. Its tone ranges from the lyric – Trinidad as an island of arresting beauty – to a seaminess of the most grungy kind. It has an ambition that challenges a novel such as V.S. Naipaul's *The Mimic Men*, but is written with the anger and the compassion of a writer for whom the island still means everything. In the novella, 'Froude's Arrow', Ramcharitar has written a profound fiction that tells us where the Caribbean currently is in juxtaposing the deep, still to be answered questions about island existence (the fragmentations wrought by history, the challenges of smallness in the global market, race and class divides) and the scrabbling for survival, fame and fortune that arouse the ire of Ramcharitar's acerbic and satirical vision.